Enjoy my book!

A Little Duck Tale

written and illustrated by
Greta Stapf Waterman

Published by Artblend Inc.
2736 East Oakland Park Blvd.
Fort Lauderdale, FL 33306 USA
www.artblend.com

A Little Duck Tale
Written & Illustrated by Greta Stapf Waterman

Greta Stapf Waterman
www.artgreta.com
gsw222@gmail.com

Printed in South Korea

First Edition Printing - May 2014
44 Pages, 16 Illustrations

CPSIA LABEL
Production Date: April 2014
Plant & Location: Printed by WeSP Printer, Gyeonggi-do, South Korea
Job / Batch # 41426-0

ISBN: 978-0-615-98012-6

A Little Duck Tale

artblend.

About the book

The duckling story was a spontaneous effort. My husband dumped these two ducklings on me when a business friend saved them from the highway and gave them to him since we "live in the country." The story describes my trials and tribulations as I set out to find information to care for them. At two in the morning, awakened by their screeching "peep, peep, peeps," my frustration mounted and the prose just flowed.

About the author/illustrator

An accomplished artist from New York City, Greta has had numerous solo and group shows in SoHo, Chelsea, as well as in various other galleries on Long Island, and in other states – California, Florida, Washington, D.C., and Santa Fe, New Mexico. She has also shown in France where she received "Mellieur Colorist" presented by then mayor and future president of France, Mssr. Jacques Chirac, at the 8th Grand Prix Fine Art de Paris, Salon de Vieux Colombier, Paris, France. Another featured achievement includes Unicef Recognition for Presentation Booklet of 10 World Artists European Distribution. As a working artist for the past few decades, Greta was approached by friend and well-known author Susan Shapiro Barash to illustrate her two newest books, "The New Wife" and "The Men Out There." This propelled others to seek her out to illustrate other works, including Frances Hill's" Such Men are Dangerous: The Fanatics of 1692 and 2004". After being inspired to create a children's book on her own based on a true event, expect more stories to come that will be fun and informative as well as educational.

Two little ducklings
dodging traffic,
picked up one day
and transferred
to their new abode.

Mother and son

on the computer,

finding out info

to see how to care

for ducks on the go.

They learned that the two

as common wild ducks –

with big webbed feet

and a broad fat bill –

are called mallards:

a drake for a he

and a hen for a she.

Marshes, bogs and sloughs

are their homes of choice,

with vegetable matter

and insects to eat.

Two wading pools were made

and a red lamp for heat;

an eating area also

and towels in a heap.

All this in a Jacuzzi –

their new place to sleep.

Show and tell at school

went over quite well –

each class had a chance

to take their own peek.

It was all so swell

with lots of learning to keep.

The next step was

the Wildlife Refuge...

but no, not yet would they take them

until the feathers set in.

So back the ducklings went;

this time an outdoor pen was made

to be their daytime tent.

17

And so the routine went
outside during the day,
where the little ducklings
could run around and play.
Back inside for the night
in the big bathtub,
curled up together
nice and tight.

Poor mom everyday
did all of the cleaning,
anxiously awaiting
to begin with the weaning.

Washing and fixing,

changing towels,

water and food –

what a mess!

Smelly and noisy

did indeed

set the mood.

Lo and behold,

a feather can be seen!

The process has started

we can begin to wean.

Look how they've grown,

the transition will begin,

for as we know

they were only on loan.

Oh dear,
oh me oh my,
with a great big sigh.
One of the ducklings
has died...

24

...trying to escape,

I guess,

and now laid down

for eternal rest.

This does happen,

as you shall see,

and life goes on

as it should be.

Which is one reason why

Mother Nature often breeds

more than a few –

up to 15 or so –

since so many

are on the go.

This leaves us with the one.

And without the mate,

it's just not as much fun...

so off to the refuge we go.

But even there,

we have some woe:

the ducklings they just got in

are certainly not his twin –

same breed but different species

or is it the other way around?

The same age

but twice as big,

and they're pecking the little guy.

Our guy is a little black duck

and the twenty others are brown & white;

certainly ready to give a good fight.

So off we go

back home to our safe abode,

where calls are made

to place our little load.

He needs his friends
and needs them quick,
he ought not get used to people,
he needs his own pick.

An interesting nature lover

was found.

She has so much wildlife –

deer, squirrel and ducklings –

all on her ground.

So off he goes

to meet the others,

hopefully more so

like his brothers.

We'll get the call
when transition is made
and they all peep together
to go off and wade.
First is an enclosed area
to start the greeting,
then learning together
for the proper meeting.
And for a while
they learn to get along,
growing their feathers
and peeping in a song.

Soon it is time

to go out in the wild –

to eat pond weed

and perhaps some seed –

released to a lake

which is best

for all their sake.

Farewell and be well,

it was all so swell

to have a quick learning –

yet we'll give up the yearning

as the ducklings go wild,

for wild ducks they are...

and it all started

in front of a car.

THE END

Draw Your Duck!